EPHEMERAL NIGHT SKIES

HANIA SHAIKH

AURAQ

Printed in the Islamic Republic of Pakistan.

Printed: March, 2021
Edition: 1st
ISBN: 978-969-749-090-5
Price: Rs 1000 PKR, $10 US

AURAQ
PUBLICATIONS

ISLAMABAD, PAKISTAN

raabta@auraqpublications.com | +92-300-0571-530
www.auraqpublications.com | @AuraqPublications

ISBN : 978-969-749-090-5

Printed and Bound by **Passive Printers** - www.passiveprinters.com

ACKNOWLEDGEMENTS

I would like to thank all of my readers, my family, and my overenthusiastic friends who have encouraged me on this journey. I would like to thank everyone except my 10th grade English teacher who reprimanded me for being "good for nothing." Well, the tables have turned.

But Ma'am, I still don't like you.

CONTENTS

27. Hey strange friend
28. You click
29. Butterflies
30. Comfortable silence
31. Silence and storm
32. Habits
33. Amber eyes
34. Silver lining
35. Ad infinitum

Dark____**43-106**

1. Everything or nothing
2. Glass crown
3. Odyssey
4. Unrequited
5. Want and won't
6. Last first thing
7. Second chances
8. If I could I would
9. Wordless
10. You without me
11. Save your breath
12. A way out
13. Home
14. Falling out of love
15. Scarlet letters
16. Code red
17. Moonchild
18. You were here first

LIGHT

The thing about poetry is

you never know the answers of who, why, and what

your first guess is hardly the right answer

but don't let me ruin the surprise for you

I won't gift wrap the answer for you

you could think of it for a lover

and it might just be for my grandma

you could think of it as a friend

and keep it by your side

I won't correct you

in fact I'd learn another way of reading it

it might remind you of something more personal

and all I hope is my words only leave good vibes

think of it however you like

it's yours now

just like I am.

-    *This is your doughnut song*

And even when everything

was going wrong

I had my writings to hold on.

-    *Scripturient*

Be vary of what you say

the force of your words

can build someone's world or

tear it all down.

The same bricks that can be used

to raise an empire

can also bring its walls tumbling down.

-    *Ominous words*

I've learnt kindness from the cruel

patience from the intolerant

love from the heartless.

I've learnt wisdom from the fool

truth from the liar and

bravery from the craven.

-    *Essence of existence*

In this fast-paced world

where nothing is enough

there's a strange solace in kindness

it multiplies by a thousand folds

and indubitably finds its way home.

You might never know the magnitude of your smile

on a shattered heart or

a word of comfort on a poignant soul

it takes nothing from you

it might mean everything to them.

- *Be kind to kind*

Can we go there where the beaches are always blue

and the sand between our toes

glimmer with a golden hue?

Can we go there where the clouds mate

and the gentles drops of rain

wash away all the pain?

Can we go there where the sun never sinks in

and the skies are crystal clear

like dazzling pale sapphires?

Can we go there where hearts feel the same

where love and kindness win

and folks rejoice in their own skin?

Can we go there where the stars are like amethysts

and the moon that hangs in the sky

ends the darkness in a cause of delight?

Can we go there? *Can we?*

-   *Can we go there?*

It's a car in which you must

take the driving seat, my dear

the chaperone next to you on the shotgun

will soon leave at his destination

and so will the passengers at the back of the car

but you mustn't stop and drive all the way

down the highway and up the hill

along the viaduct and if the car breaks down

near an abandoned mill

don't despair and find a solution, you never fail

you'll carry on for the journey is not done

despite the hindrances and trivial storms

you'll find plenty of inns to sojourn

sometimes you'll be lost only to start over again

but be the driver yourself through thick and thin

don't pass the wheel to anyone under any constrain.

-    *Life is a car*

Don't just sit there

waiting for a better world

kingdoms have fallen, wallowing in sad dreams.

Don't believe the lies

just because it's easier to believe them

see the world as it is

not how you want it to be and do your part to change it

and in doing so, start by changing yourself

little by little, seconds for minutes

it's within not without.

We don't build the boat at the storm's arrival

start small now, go far.

You hold the trigger of your gun

the key to your car

the rein of your charge

nothing comes free in this world

least of all freedom.

-    *Onwards and upwards*

We all walk through the flames

what matters is how well we walk

we all die a hundred times in a relatively short life

what matters is how well was the one time we lived

we all fail through and through

what matters is how well we fail

we all fall a million times

what matters is how well we rise again.

-    *Resilience*

Ask the value of a roof from the person

sleeping sprawl-eagled on the pavement

his blanket is the cold, his ceiling is star-strewn.

Ask the worth of life from the man

on the brink of death

for he will give you the right answer

when no one else can

he will tell you what a wonderful blessing it is

to have a throbbing heart

he will savour his every breath

for any could be his last.

-    *Worth*

She left stars in her wake

and paved the road with her smiles

making the darkest souls burn bright.

She loves the sunrise

because it tells her

however dark the night is

it always end.

She loves the sunset

because it reminds her

the ending could be

just as pretty.

-    *Beginnings and endings*

Everything ends

every smile fades

every heart breaks

but you must carry on

if a drop from the ocean goes missing

the ocean doesn't stop.

Don't despair, I promise

whatever's hurting you today

will become a story for the weekends

you'll rise again for

every sorrow also passes

every heart heals

every dawn breaks.

-    *Darling, it's all ephemeral*

Just like a rainbow follows

a torrential downpour

the happiness is truly felt

after a long night of deep sorrow.

For without winter

what would be the value of spring?

-    *Something good this way comes*

Perhaps we need to suffer a little

to strengthen.

We're like glass, all of us

perhaps we need to break a little

leaving the cracks open

for light to enter.

- *Glass half full*

They say there's light

at the end of every tunnel

although the length of the tunnel

is never guaranteed.

-	*Hang in there*

She was cold as ice

and sedate as poison

she was hot-headed

like the Vesuvius

and still as water

she was everything

and nothing

she never asked for a throne

or a crown

only a longsword

things didn't go right for her

they went *wrong*

so with spurs

she trampled upon those plights

with the force of a raging storm.

-    *And like that she became a knight*

The hands that wipe the tears

are nonpareil to the lips that kiss the smile.

Hearts woven in despair are stronger

than temporary strings of happiness and health.

-    *Laces*

Give me all your broken parts

and I'll sew them back together

I can't promise they'll be good as new

but they'll make do.

Give me your wretched heart

and I'll build a kingdom out of it

in your lonely yard

but like every kingdom it'll rise and fall

sometimes it'll be broken

sometimes stand tall.

-    *Stand tall*

When you are with me avoid being somebody else

it's elementary for me to find cracks in the mirror.

-    *Be you*

There are several false standards of beauty

but if you ask me what true beauty is?

It's in the scars that you earned

after falling from the stairs when you were young

it's in hiding your mother's favourite vase

that you broke in your haste

it's in getting whiff of the same fragrance that your

grandfather used to wear from a mere stranger

it's in your dishevelled hair and lined clothes

and in the ink blotches on your fingers

as you frantically scribble down your notes

it's in the mark on your cheek that poxes left you

and in the croak of your morning voice

it's in the messed up writing

on the last page of your exam sheet

and the way you laugh at your own joke.

-      *The beauty is in the beast in you*

You're a star that glows in the dark

shine, even if the skies fall apart

you're a lotus surrounded with the dirt

shine and never lose your worth

you're a moth that flies near the flames

shine, even if it hurts like hell

you're a boat that sails against the wind

shine and go all in

you're an angel in a human suit

shine and never lose your wings

shine, just shine

and never let the world steal your smile.

-    *Shine*

Give me all your sins and lies

your flaws and your blemishes.

Give me not just your perfect disposition

but your wild temperament

for that's what makes you human in my eyes.

-   *Human*

Your scars are not your baggage

let them define you

wear them with *bloody* pride

they're some of your finest jewels

that depict your inner conquests

and the triumphs of your skin

they show how far you've travelled

and how many miles are still left

they show that a new dawn came for you

after every starless night.

-    *Baggage*

A sculpture goes through innumerable stages

to look perfect.

If you're looking for flawlessness

are you sure you're not looking for carved stone?

-    *Sculpture*

Who's the first person you think of when I say

someone who's full of life?

Now hold on to that picture in your mind's eye

and make a promise to yourself that

you'll never lose them

for they make you feel alive.

-   *Picture perfect*

That I thought was the difference between

everyone else and her.

I was known for my witty comebacks

and for having the last word

so naturally I mocked her

but her sardonic retorts were of equal measure

and in that instance I knew I found my equal.

-    *That's how we became friends*

I'm forever grateful for the day we met

inhabitants of two worlds

broke their ranks

you thought I was strange

I definitely thought you were so

but despite all these polarities

we stayed through the sands of time

the coincidences or whatever they were

made me question the indolence of the universe

or there was a science beyond those coincidences

whatever it was

hey strange friend, remember

even when I'm not with you

I'm with you.

-     *Hey strange friend*

Sometimes it takes half a heartbeat

for someone to click

and sometimes an eternity

is not enough.

-    *You click*

I never had the heart to tell you

that the poetry you fawned over

was written only for you.

-      *Butterflies*

When I realized

sitting in silence with you

wasn't uncomfortable at all

I knew you were the one.

-    *Comfortable silence*

His love was silent

like a starless night

when it showed

it showed in little things.

Her love was wild

like the bluest ocean

when it came

it came like a storm.

-    *Silence and storm*

If you haven't loved someone to the point

where their habits starts growing on you

you haven't loved enough.

-    *Habits*

My numb toes graze the edge of no tomorrow.

These watery depths do not affright me

for I've already drowned a million times

in your eyes.

-    *Amber eyes*

It's hot, it's cold, like fire meets ice

tempers run high, breathing shallow

you feast, you flame

thorns on rose

it's a yin-yang: black in white, white in black

circles have no end, they begin where they end

night and day, light and dark

like a silver lining we are

the whispers, the screams

it's our heaven, our hell

you shrine, you sanctuary

friend or foe, ally or enemy

you blessing, you curse

war or peace, sleep or death

angel with the broken wings or

the devil with a crown on his head

who do you think you are?

-    *Silver lining*

We keep coming back, don't we?

we keep going in endless circles

but anytime you feel like

you want an out, just say it aloud

but if you'll leave the door open

I promise, I'll leave the door open.

-    *Ad infinitum*

DARK

Go take your time

let the morning breeze

kiss away your tears

let the sun cast its light

upon the sins of your skin.

Take your time

but when you come back

come back wholeheartedly.

I want all of you

or none of you.

-    *Everything or nothing*

Hania Shaikh

You were my crown

but you were made of glass

and no amount of delicacy

could've saved you from falling

from my eyes

I tried to handle the broken shards

but they simply left a hole in my heart.

-     *Glass crown*

Just when the docks neared

a wave was all it took to devour us.

We voyaged an ocean

only to drown in the shallows.

-    *Odyssey*

You too should love like us

you too should burn like us.

-    *Unrequited*

And who told you that the extent of love

could be quantifiable by busts of porcelain?

By monuments of sleek stone?

You gave her the world

but maybe, *just maybe*

she only wanted you.

-    *Want and won't*

Hania Shaikh

You don't know how to leave

I don't know how to stay.

Meeting you was the next best thing

that happened to me.

Losing you was the first.

-    *Last first thing*

Broke all promises

changed my number

I never answered your call

set it all on fire

drove down, singing along to

"Hey Jude" on my amplifier.

It was a one way down road

with a point of no return

I never gave you a second chance

never looked back once.

-    *Second chances*

I never intend on losing you

I was too busy finding myself.

The note of plea, the need to self-explain

still rings in my head

in the most unwelcoming times:

"This heart isn't meant to love, it's meant to be free."

-    *If I could I would*

This eerie silence beseech me:

"What is worse?"

Losing someone after knowing them or

never knowing them enough to lose?

What a shame for a person who gambles with words

to be finally at lost for once.

-    *Wordless*

Can the scent be separated from the flower?

Can the heart have any worth without its beating?

In this bleakness, without me

you're a leafless tree.

Bury me with all my memories, I dare you

there's no escape from this disease.

For a flower fallen from a branch

will only wither and rot.

-    *You without me*

What you call perfection

I call satisfactory.

Darling, you're some*thing* else

and I'm some*one* else entirely.

- *Save your breath*

Heard you found a way out

heard you finally found a release

well, that makes the two of us.

- *A way out*

Never make anyone your home or

you'll be left on the streets

never make anyone your island or

you'll be left stranded

never give anyone the key to your heart or

you'll never know what tore it apart.

- *Home*

No one lives for anyone

no one dies for anyone.

Falling out of love

is as easy as falling in.

-    *Falling out of love*

The muscular organ enclosed in your ribcage

better be left at its trivial task of pumping blood

it's no good writing any name on it in scarlet letters.

Don't blame the heart

blame yourself, you rampant fool.

-    *Scarlet letters*

They say love is free

wait till they lose everything for it

and call it the most expensive thing in the world.

If you can love

there's little else you can do

and for that you have my sincerest condolences.

-    *Code red*

"I'll take you to the moon."

Why, to asphyxiate me?

Settle for something nearer home.

-     *Moonchild*

But we made some good memories, didn't we?

Had the whole world dancing at the balls of our feet

late night calls 'til our phones run dead

we never cared about the time we spent

but look at us now

detached from the world we fought so hard to build

how hard it is to stay in touch?

Months, maybe years have elapsed

waiting for a reunion that never comes to pass

texting a *'happy birthday'* once a year

if we're lucky enough to remember

but no one is to be blamed, life was running too fast

and we were just keeping up with the pace

but with all honesty, even now

when I close my eyes and place a hand on my heart

it beats, "you were here first."

- *You were here first*

We built a house from broken bones

but forgot a window for the light

we took off too fast

and forgot there's a landing for every flight

we treated the ties as manacles, holding us down

in reality they were there to keep us steady

on the uneven ground

we were too young to know

that the things we were giving up

were the things that kept us sane

too smart for our own good

and looking back, we just hope

we didn't trade happiness for what's mundane

we were looking at the things

they placed for us to see

that we forgot what was

right in front of you and me

we sailed through the seas

but the tides were too high unforeseen

we made a kite

but it was also caught up in the wind

if only they knew half of the things that we did

they would've made a mountain out of it

the cage door was ajar and we gave escape a try

who would've told us?

"Learn before you fly."

When the time for the curtain call came

we laughed like the rest

curtain closed, a smile was hard to shed

we wrote a song, but soon we realized

it wasn't the ink that marked our initials on it

we bought expensive watches

when we couldn't turn back time

and if given the second chance

we'll make the same mistakes over again

we understood the reasons that we gave

but they did nothing to heal the hearts that we've slain

we saw what we wanted to see

and promised we'd never leave

we wanted to touch the skies

but forgot some of us were afraid of heights

we had a chance and threw it in flames

we had everything and let it slide away

we promised it didn't matter

that we weren't each other's first

we were okay being last

we started a journey

ended it miles apart.

-    *Miles apart*

Hania Shaikh

The world is a cruel jape

in times of joy you find yourself

in the company of many friends

in times of sorrow

you find the real ones

in your highs

they look for you

in your lows

they run from you

when you cheer

the world is with you

in despair

you weep alone.

-     *Fake real friends*

This night gathers with thoughtless provocations

these stars shine tantalizingly

blissfully ignorant to my woeful struggle.

Dear Peace, can you be my friend?

It's hard to understand

where this stillness end and agitation begins.

-    *Dear Peace*

What kills is what gives breath

the reason of my highs

is the same as the reason of my lows

my obsession, the flame to which I'm drawn like a moth

is what burns me alive

my tranquillity and trepidation

are the two sides of the same coin

the reason of my insomnia

is the same as the reason of my intoxication

what keeps me awake at nights is also

what gives me peace of mind.

-    *Tranquillity and trepidation*

I've learnt from an early age

when I needed someone the most

I was the loneliest

when I feared the most

I was the bravest

when the tidal waves were closing in on me

I learnt to breathe

when I wanted to quit

I battled on

I've learnt the hard way a long time ago

and when I say this

you'll never find a softer heart

in an iron cage anywhere else

I mean it because

I'm a force to be reckoned with.

-    *A force to be reckoned with*

I'd rather be the prisoner of the world

I was freed from

alone in my head

the silence melting like candle wax

pressing on my eardrums

like the heavy thuds of a battle axe

the breathing lungs, the beating heart

giving testimony inside me of a living part

around my dwelling, the sheer mirth and jeers

feel alien to my silent vigil

just take it all away and leave me bare

I can no longer stand these watchful stares.

-   *Outcast*

And it's ironic that

someone can be alone in a packed crowd

but have a universe within him without a doubt.

-    *Seclusion*

There's a whirlwind of emotions in my heart

and a praiseworthy smile on my face

even in these bleak hours

when fear clouds my judgment, curls my flesh

these demons of mine I'd rather not share, thanks.

-    *Demons not for sale*

What an unusual world

the rich gets rich

buying everything that can be bought with money

and yet they frown

as though they're going to drown.

The poor has an empty pocket and a huge grin

their spirits cannot be dampened

by a little bit of rain.

-    *Strange world*

Who's living in the present these days?

Half of the people I come across

are worried for the future

putting their dreams on auction

and the other half

are stuck in the memories

of the bitter past.

-   *Auctioned dreams*

And the irony is

we read about love and life

from heartbreak and anguish.

- *Irony*

They put on a good show

but they were never on our side

the jury was rigged

we fell back from the race

it was not a war we could win

the winner was decided

the liars were applauded

the game was over

way before it began.

-     *Game over*

Mankind is doomed

for we're always attracted to the things

that kill us.

We romanticize those pages

crowning them

in a grandiose way

the chapters that should've been burned

and ripped apart.

-    *Humanity, be damned*

The civilized animals, the caged men

it was the sun's darker side none saw coming

we knew the consequences but we never behaved

"nothing happens to us," was what we said

until we were left to pray.

It was a test we were meant to fail

the early bird brought the news

the ocean played its final notes

the grass was dampened beneath the feet

the weight of it all crushed on me

with an air of false bravado

I shook my head to the ones he meant more

than he ever did to me.

"Pale as death" isn't a universal statement

was all I could think

for he looked flushed, bordering at pink

the uncanny bravery that took its hold

was of a captain whose skill is measured

by his ability to sail through the storm.

Life is a slave of death

one second you're here

and the next you're —

-    *Slave of death*

Hania Shaikh

I never saw you leave

because witnessing it would've been

the final nail in the coffin

irrevocable, irretrievable

and you know, I always run out of storage

so I deleted all your photos

thinking there'll be time, *years* for more

now all I have left are old Polaroids

with edges unkempt

and it's just another season

but your memory is already vague

as I sat to draw you out

will I ever make you right?

-   *Polaroid*

I stood at the mouth of a dark cavern

for a long while

maybe years or a thousand lifetimes

where travellers have long since lost their lives

and everything I ever wanted was on the other side.

-    *Other side*

The moment I opened my eyes

I was carried from arm to arm

I heard the scribbling of my name

on documents and birth form.

The moment I closed my eyes

I was carried from arm to arm

I heard the scratching of my name

on the headstone among the gone.

-    *In the blink of an eye*

And the one time she asked for help

they gave her a wooden sword

while flames licked every town, every herd.

Do you know what she has now become?

An echo from the past.

Have you seen the petals around her?

Will they long last?

-    *An elegy of a nyctophile*

Like a phoenix I was reborn

to turn *their* whole world into

a smouldering pile of ashes.

Should I be thanking *you*?

Well, thank you

because I began where we ended.

-    *I began where we ended*

I looked in the mirror and asked:

"Which one is it, Batman or Superman?"

and the mirror did something very strange.

It showed me my face.

-    *Mirror on the wall*

In a world

where I let them feel the joy

in the false notion of saving me

I take pride in the fact that

they wouldn't have made this far

if not for me.

-   *Sanctimony*

Some people think I have a heart of gold

some think I don't have a heart at all

they're right, all of them

but the fault isn't with me

it's with them.

-    *Unperturbed*

I'm a pathetically possessive person, you know

for the things that really matter

whether they're my stars or my scars

I whisper to them:

"Keep your shit together, there's no way I'm sharing you."

And if I really want something

I will make it mine.

-    *If I want, it's mine*

And she was made of

silk and steel

roses and thorns

she was neither hot nor cold

but lukewarm

they ignored her smiles

and focussed on the scorns

so she annihilated everything

before a semicolon.

-    *Semicolon*

Hania Shaikh

I'm like a cactus

survivor of cold nights and savage storms.

The years, however, left imprints

and now I have thorns

instead of rose.

-    *Imprints*

They lied to my face and thought they had me

I played along with them because

revealing their lies was way below me.

-      *Eminence*

How naïve you have to be

to think your little lies will work with me?

I've been in your place before

know a fake smile when I see one

I've been doing it for a while, love.

Can see through your smiling eyes

right into your rainbow heart

but wait, no concept of black and white?

Shady, just shady

grey is where we reside.

You thought you'd play the game?

Play it, love, and play it well

because I'm already waiting by the finish line

in this game, the rules are mine.

-    *White lies*

All the lies I've told

all the lives I've lived

different people, same day

making sure none overlap

it's exhausting being in my head

when the curtains open and the stage is set

new day, new role

no worries, new stories

with none the wiser than the rest.

You don't know me

you only know the part of me

that I want you to know.

All the lines I've learnt, what if I mix them?

Let's keep the fences, shall we?

And do it all over again.

-    *Fences*

The smiling eyes thwarted

no one separated the false and the truth

some smile at the face and stab in the back

some present flowers, pretty in sight

only to turn out as Daphne with death lurking inside

they always come with open hearts

white as saints, but then again

in chess, who starts the game?

-    *Sinners as saints*

I despise the sinners in the guise of saints

but nothing infuriates me more than fools

swallowing their tall tales.

-    *Tall tales*

Known enemies I understand, even admire

these are the snakes in my sleeves that I repel.

In this grey world

where everyone is busy playing the saint

if we're evil, then evil it is.

-    *Serpents*

You can't win a horse race on foot

you can't clean filth

and not expect to have dirt on your hands

you can't win their game

without playing it by their rules

you play by the book, they don't

and that's why they'll always be better than you.

They say wipe dirt with a rag

clean towel is such a waste

and with that being said

I hope you know what to do next.

-    *Brave new world*

There's only one way to go

for those who reach the mountain top

and it's down.

The fall is always hard

for the ones who fly high.

\-   *The fall*

Power

it corrupts us all.

A poison disguised as elixir

an endless desire

a perilous intoxication

an eternal damnation.

One taste of this mulled wine

and no one looks for sobriety again.

-    *Power; poison or elixir?*

If you ask them

I'd be the villain in their story

a witch they wanted to bury

but they'll never set me on fire

a vain desire

for they know they need me

know I need them not

so set me aflame

I cannot be tamed

or find someone else to blame.

- *Tame*

Princesses bore me

pathetic little things

always getting into trouble

waiting to be saved.

Witches ensnare me

with their lethal stares

their every word weighed carefully

like a sweet spell

waiting to be set loose

to wreak havoc, wake hell

their touch electrocutes

like a knife in the heart

twisting slowly like a kiss of nightshade.

Honey, I don't want to rule your dreams

I want to haunt your nightmares.

- *Honey, I want to be a pretty witch*

Wasn't it great, meeting their expectations?

Being exactly what they called her

leaving no room for human errors.

She wished she was half an inch of the monster

they thought she was

they portrayed her as the villain

and since she was always considerate of what they thought

so she became one

completing their story.

-    *I like this script*

And you were kind, weren't you?

And buoyant

and loud

you laughed easily

but went quieter in the way

more subdued

more you.

How long will it take you to become

what you fought against?

-    *Rear view*

I still walk the same road

I still play the same notes

and it occurs to me like a vivid dream

a life that hardly seems my own

all the naivety buried deep

to the miles I've walked

so much could happen between now and then

nothing is permanent.

If I had told my old self

that in years to come this is what I'd become

would I've believed?

What if I'm the one thing I never wanted to be?

-    *A walk down to an old country lane*

I maybe the victor of war

but I'm the result of several failed battles.

There comes a time

in all of our lives

when we wonder

whether the choices we made

were even worth making.

That whether the end really

justifies the means.

-    *This is my time*

And those paper dreams I had

were not meant to last

in search for the skies

I've lost my stars.

   -   *Paper dreams*